Grammar Practice Book

Teacher Edition
Grade 3

Harcourt

Visit *The Learning Site!*
www.harcourtschool.com

ISBN 10 0-15-349916-8
ISBN 13 978-0-15-349916-6

3 4 5 6 7 8 9 10   073   12 11 10 09 08 07

Contents

Name _____

▲ Rewrite each group of words to form a
statement that makes sense. Use capital letters
and end marks correctly.

1. Vaughn on Maple Street lives
   Vaughn lives on Maple Street.

2. he a student new is
   He is a new student.

3. math he enjoys
   He enjoys math.

4. flute the he plays
   He plays the flute.

5. from London is Andrea
   Andrea is from London.

6. science she good is at
   She is good at science.

7. lives she near park the
   She lives near the park.

8. she likes dance to
   She likes to dance.

9. teaches Mr. Jackson third grade
   Mr. Jackson teaches third grade.

10. He the welcomes children new
    He welcomes the new children.

1

Name _____

▲ Rewrite each group of words to form a question that makes sense. Use capital letters and end marks correctly.

1. you do a brother have
   Do you have a brother?

2. what his name is
   What is his name?

3. he to school go does
   Does he go to school?

4. he read can
   Can he read?

5. play he does where
   Where does he play?

▲ Turn each statement into a question. Use the word in parentheses ( ) as the first word. Possible responses are shown.

6. My little sister's name is Sara. (What)
   What is your little sister's name?

7. She copies everything I do. (Why)
   Why does she copy everything you do?

8. She meets me after school. (When)
   When does she meet you?

9. She wants to go to the store. (Where)
   Where does she want to go?

Name _____

▲ Read this part of a student's rough draft. Then answer the questions that follow.

(1) I to like skip. (2) Why do I skip (3) it is more fun than walking. (4) I skip all the way to school (5) With my friends at recess. (6) _____ you like to skip, too?

1. In which sentence are the words in an order that does NOT make sense?
   Ⓐ Sentence 1
   B Sentence 2
   C Sentence 4
   D Sentence 5

2. Which sentence does not tell a complete thought?
   A Sentence 1
   B Sentence 3
   C Sentence 4
   Ⓓ Sentence 5

3. Which sentence should end with a question mark?
   Ⓐ Sentence 2
   B Sentence 3
   C Sentence 4
   D Sentence 5

4. Which sentence is missing a period?
   A Sentence 1
   B Sentence 2
   Ⓒ Sentence 4
   D Sentence 5

5. Which word in Sentence 3 should be capitalized?
   A is
   Ⓑ it
   C way
   D fun

6. Which word would make sense in the blank in Sentence 6?
   A Why
   B But
   Ⓒ Do
   D Where

Name _____

▲ Add the correct end mark to each sentence.
Then label each as a *statement* or a *question.*

1. Where is the teacher __?__ ___question___

2. I do not like to jump __.__ ___statement___

3. When does Anita run __?__ ___question___

4. Do you know Mr. Wang __?__ ___question___

5. We play in the grass __.__ ___statement___

▲ Rewrite each group of words to form a statement or a
question. Put the words in an order that makes sense.
Use capital letters and end marks correctly.

6. to the park I go (statement)
   ___I go to the park.___

7. do walk you to school (question)
   ___Do you walk to school?___

8. Willow ball the throws (statement)
   ___Willow throws the ball.___

9. can Kurt play softball (statement)
   ___Kurt can play softball.___

10. you can football play (question)
    ___Can you play football?___

Name _____

▲ Rewrite each sentence, using capital letters and
end marks correctly. Then label each as a *command*
or an *exclamation.*

1. give the book to Violet
   ___Give the book to Violet.; command___

2. what a great author he is
   ___What a great author he is!; exclamation___

3. how excited I am to read his new story
   ___How excited I am to read his new story!; exclamation___

4. let your brother read
   ___Let your brother read.; command___

5. oops, I lost the book
   ___Oops, I lost the book!; exclamation___

6. help me find it
   ___Help me find it.; command___

7. search in the living room
   ___Search in the living room.; command___

8. wow, it is a mess in here
   ___Wow, it is a mess in here!; exclamation___

9. hurray, here it is
   ___Hurray, here it is!; exclamation___

10. look at the pretty cover
    ___Look at the pretty cover.; command___

Name _____

▲ Rewrite each sentence, using capital letters and end marks correctly. Then label each as a *statement*, a *question*, a *command*, or an *exclamation*.

1. Cathy wants to be a writer
   Cathy wants to be a writer.; statement

2. read Cathy's story
   Read Cathy's story.; command

3. what does she write about
   What does she write about?; question

4. what a good writer Cathy is
   What a good writer Cathy is!; exclamation

▲ Add words and end marks to make four kinds of sentences out of the words in the box. **Possible responses are shown.**

the	things	Cathy	does

5. a question
   What are the things Cathy does?

6. a statement
   These are the things Cathy does.

7. an exclamation
   Wow, the things Cathy does are exciting!

8. a command
   Think about the things Cathy does.

Name _____

▲ Read this part of a student's rough draft. Then answer the questions that follow.

(1) Wow, today was an exciting day. (2) What an interesting time we had (3) A firefighter visited our school. (4) Our teacher how to prepare. (5) She told us to think of questions to ask the firefighter (6) What question do you think I asked.

1. Which sentence should end with an exclamation point?
   (A) Sentence 1
   B Sentence 4
   C Sentence 5
   D Sentence 6

2. Which sentence should end with a question mark?
   A Sentence 1
   B Sentence 3
   C Sentence 4
   (D) Sentence 6

3. Which end mark should Sentence 2 have?
   A a period
   B a comma
   C a question mark
   (D) an exclamation point

4. Which end mark should Sentence 5 have?
   (A) a period
   B a comma
   C a question mark
   D an exclamation point

5. Which sentence is not complete?
   A Sentence 1
   B Sentence 3
   (C) Sentence 4
   D Sentence 6

6. Which sentence is correct?
   A Sentence 2
   (B) Sentence 3
   C Sentence 4
   D Sentence 6

Name _____

▲ If the sentence is complete, add a correct end mark. If the sentence is not complete, write *not a sentence*. **Possible responses are shown.**

1. My father is an author ____ .

2. How he loves to write ____ !

3. How do I help him ____ ?

4. Things that he can write about ___ not a sentence

5. Read his latest book ____ .

6. Wow, it's exciting ____ !

▲ Add words and end marks to make four kinds of sentences. Each sentence is started for you. **Possible responses are shown.**

7. a statement
You have brown eyes.

8. a command
Go to school.

9. an exclamation
What a nice day it is!

10. a question
What are you doing?

Name _____

▲ Underline the simple subject. Write the predicate.

1. Lisa went to boarding school.
went to boarding school

2. My good friend learned at home.
learned at home

3. He rode the bus to school.
rode the bus to school

4. His older sister studied dance.
studied dance

5. I went to school.
went to school

6. Leroy enjoyed college.
enjoyed college

7. The high school student worked on Sundays.
worked on Sundays

8. Dad helped my brother.
helped my brother

9. The little girl painted pictures.
painted pictures

Try This

Choose four sentences from a book or magazine. Write the sentences. Underline the simple subjects. **Accept reasonable responses.**

Name _____

▲ Underline the complete predicate. Write the simple predicate.

1. Hannah likes math.
   likes

2. Science is my favorite subject.
   is

3. Jamil studies French every day.
   studies

4. My cousin wears a uniform to school.
   wears

5. The teacher plans her lesson carefully.
   plans

6. The boys clean their desks.
   clean

7. The children read quietly.
   read

8. Some students use a computer.
   use

9. Everyone enjoys the class trip.
   enjoys

10. Valerie practices the trumpet.
    practices

Name _____

▲ Read this part of a student's rough draft. Then answer the questions that follow.

(1) My little brother is five years old. (2) He goes to kindergarten. (3) Kindergarten fun. (4) The young children learn with toys and games.

1. Which is the complete subject of Sentence 1?
   A My little
   B brother
   C My little brother
   D is five years old

2. Which is the complete predicate of Sentence 1?
   A is
   B five years old
   C My little brother
   D is five years old

3. Which is the simple subject of Sentence 2?
   A He goes
   B to kindergarten
   C He
   D goes

4. Which is the simple predicate of Sentence 2?
   A He
   B goes
   C goes to kindergarten
   D to kindergarten

5. Which is the complete subject of Sentence 4?
   A The young children
   B children
   C children learn
   D learn

6. Which sentence does NOT have a correct predicate?
   A Sentence 1
   B Sentence 2
   C Sentence 3
   D Sentence 4

Complete and Simple Subjects and Predicates
Lesson 3

▲ Add a complete subject to each predicate. Then underline the simple subject. **Possible responses are shown.**

1. The good student went to school.
2. Three boys played outside.
3. The hungry children ate lunch.
4. The little girl took a nap.
5. Some dancers performed on stage.
6. The new house was made of brick.

▲ Add a complete predicate to each subject. Then underline the simple predicate. **Possible responses are shown.**

7. An art teacher came to our classroom
8. The excited children jumped up and down
9. He walked to the store
10. My mother helped me study
11. The school was on the corner
12. The tired baby closed her eyes

▲ Rewrite each pair of sentences as one sentence. Draw one line under each compound subject and two lines under each compound predicate.

1. Juan played the piano. His sister played the piano.
   Juan and his sister played the piano.

2. The children worked hard. The children practiced every day.
   The children worked hard and practiced every day.

3. Music filled the room. Laughter filled the room.
   Music and laughter filled the room.

4. Michelle wanted to write poems. Diego wanted to write poems.
   Michelle and Diego wanted to write poems.

5. They wrote in their notebooks. They studied with a teacher.
   They wrote in their notebooks and studied with a teacher.

6. My uncle went to school. My uncle learned to cook.
   My uncle went to school and learned to cook.

7. Carmen loved soccer. Her cousin loved soccer.
   Carmen and her cousin loved soccer.

8. They played together. They won trophies.
   They played together and won trophies.

9. Mr. Han's students talked. Mr. Han's students made plans.
   Mr. Han's students talked and made plans.

Compound Subjects and Predicates
Lesson 4

▲ Write the compound subject of each sentence. Add commas where they belong.

1. Ravi his grandmother and his grandfather went to the school concert.
   Ravi, his grandmother, and his grandfather

2. Ravi's teacher his neighbor and his friend were in the audience.
   Ravi's teacher, his neighbor, and his friend

3. The violins cellos and flutes sounded beautiful.
   The violins, cellos, and flutes

4. The drums cymbals and gong played an exciting ending.
   The drums, cymbals, and gong

5. A tall woman a short man and a child left the hall first.
   A tall woman, a short man, and a child

▲ Write the compound predicate of each sentence. Add commas where they belong.

6. Ravi went home changed into pajamas and climbed into bed.
   went home, changed into pajamas, and climbed into bed

7. He lay down fell asleep and dreamed he was a musician.
   lay down, fell asleep, and dreamed he was a musician

8. He played a solo bowed and smiled at the audience.
   played a solo, bowed, and smiled at the audience

9. The audience stood up clapped and cheered.
   stood up, clapped, and cheered

Grammar-Writing Connection
Lesson 4

▲ Read this part of a student's rough draft. Then answer the questions that follow.

(1) Madeline and Ella were sisters. (2) They wanted to be doctors when they grew up. (3) Their mother shared their goal. (4) Their father shared their goal. (5) The girls worked hard and got good grades. (6) They got into a special school succeeded and became doctors.

1. Which sentence has a compound subject?
   Ⓐ Sentence 1
   B Sentence 2
   C Sentence 5
   D Sentence 6

2. Which sentence needs commas to separate the compound predicates?
   A Sentence 1
   B Sentence 2
   C Sentence 5
   Ⓓ Sentence 6

3. Which sentences could be joined to make one sentence with a compound subject?
   A Sentences 2 and 3
   Ⓑ Sentences 3 and 4
   C Sentences 4 and 5
   D Sentences 5 and 6

4. Which sentence has a compound predicate that is written correctly?
   A Sentence 1
   B Sentence 3
   Ⓒ Sentence 5
   D Sentence 6

5. Which of these sentences does NOT have a compound subject or a compound predicate?
   A Sentence 1
   Ⓑ Sentence 2
   C Sentence 5
   D Sentence 6

6. Which of these possible final sentences has a compound subject?
   A Their dream came true.
   Ⓑ The sisters and their parents had a dream that came true.
   C They healed and cured.
   D People admired them.

Name _____

Compound Subjects and Predicates
Lesson 4

▲ Add a compound subject or a compound predicate to complete each sentence.

Possible responses are shown.

1. Rita and Max _____ studied art.

2. The athletes ran and swam _____.

3. The music student practiced and performed _____.

4. Elena and her best friend _____ took dance classes.

5. The actor smiled and waved _____.

6. The boy and girl _____ watched the stars.

▲ Rewrite each sentence. Add commas where they belong. Draw one line under each compound subject and two lines under each compound predicate.

7. The soccer player ran kicked and scored.
   The soccer player ran, kicked, and scored.

8. Exercise rest and healthful food made the swimmer strong.
   Exercise, rest, and healthful food made the swimmer strong.

9. Raja his sister and his brother were good students.
   Raja, his sister, and his brother were good students.

10. The scientist wrote a book won a prize and gave a speech.
    The scientist wrote a book, won a prize, and gave a speech.

Name _____

Grammar–Writing Connection
Lesson 5

▲ Read this part of a student's rough draft. Then answer the questions that follow.

(1) There is something new in Room 112 (2) Can you guess what it is (3) our rabbit has four babies. (4) How tiny the bunnies are! (5) Wish could take one home. (6) Do you bunnies like?

1. Which sentence should end with a period?
   (A) Sentence 1
   B Sentence 2
   C Sentence 4
   D Sentence 6

2. Which sentence should end with a question mark?
   A Sentence 1
   (B) Sentence 2
   C Sentence 3
   D Sentence 4

3. In which sentence are the words in an order that does not make sense?
   A Sentence 2
   B Sentence 3
   C Sentence 4
   (D) Sentence 6

4. Which word in Sentence 3 should be capitalized?
   (A) our
   B rabbit
   C four
   D babies

5. Which of the following is NOT a complete sentence?
   A Sentence 1
   B Sentence 3
   C Sentence 4
   (D) Sentence 5

6. Which sentence is correct as it is?
   A Sentence 3
   (B) Sentence 4
   C Sentence 5
   D Sentence 6

▲ Read this part of a student's rough draft.
Then answer the questions that follow.

(1) Eric watched the news on TV. (2) His father
watched the news on TV. (3) The newscaster talked
about special events. (4) A police officer a firefighter
and a teacher taught third graders about safety. (5) The
mayor took a trip and gave a speech.

1. Which is the simple subject of
   Sentence 1?
   Ⓐ Eric
   B Eric watched
   C the news
   D watched the news on TV

2. Which is the complete
   predicate of Sentence 3?
   A the newscaster
   B the newscaster talked
   C talked
   Ⓓ talked about special events

3. What is missing in Sentence 4?
   Ⓐ commas
   B a subject
   C a simple predicate
   D a complete predicate

4. Which sentence has a
   compound subject?
   A Sentence 1
   B Sentence 3
   Ⓒ Sentence 4
   D Sentence 5

5. Which sentence has a
   compound predicate?
   A Sentence 2
   B Sentence 3
   C Sentence 4
   Ⓓ Sentence 5

6. Which sentences could be
   joined to make one sentence
   with a compound subject?
   Ⓐ Sentences 1 and 2
   B Sentences 2 and 3
   C Sentences 3 and 4
   D Sentences 4 and 5

▲ If the sentence is complete, label it as *simple* or
compound. If it is a fragment, add words to make
it complete. **Possible responses are shown for 2, 5, and 10.**

1. My big sister has a job.
   simple

2. After school.
   She works after school.

3. She works at a pet store.
   simple

4. She feeds the animals, and she cleans their cages.
   compound

5. Sweeps the floor.
   She sweeps the floor.

6. My sister enjoys her job, but she also likes weekends.
   compound

7. She spends time with friends, or she relaxes at home.
   compound

8. My brother is sixteen, and he works on weekends.
   compound

9. He packs bags at a supermarket.
   simple

10. My family.
    My family is happy.

Name

Simple and Compound Sentences
Lesson 6

▲ **Use the words in the parentheses ( ) to join the pairs of sentences. Use commas correctly.**

1. Today is Sunday. Andy goes to a football game. (and)
Today is Sunday, and Andy goes to a football game.

2. He is excited. He eats breakfast quickly. (and)
He is excited, and he eats breakfast quickly.

3. Linda wants to go with Andy. She is sick. (but)
Linda wants to go with Andy, but she is sick.

4. Andy's mother goes to the game. His father stays home. (but)
Andy's mother goes to the game, but his father stays home.

5. Tanya has strong legs. She loves to run. (and)
Tanya has strong legs, and she loves to run.

6. She likes softball. She likes basketball more. (but)
She likes softball, but she likes basketball more.

7. Some children play in the gym. Anna plays in the park. (but)
Some children play in the gym, but Anna plays in the park.

8. It is a hot day. Children sell lemonade. (and)
It is a hot day, and children sell lemonade.

9. Darnell likes lemonade. He likes milk more. (but)
Darnell likes lemonade, but he likes milk more.

10. He walks to the store. He buys milk. (and)
He walks to the store, and he buys milk.

Name

Grammar-Writing Connection
Lesson 6

▲ **Read this part of a student's rough draft. Then answer the questions that follow.**

(1) Maya is a third grader, or she helps her family. (2) She washes the dishes, and she waters the plants. (3) Also cleans her room. (4) Maya's father makes breakfast most mornings. (5) Today he leaves early for work. (6) Maya's brother cooks eggs, he serves them to his family.

1. Which sentence is NOT complete?
A Sentence 2
B Sentence 3
C Sentence 4
D Sentence 5

2. Which sentence is a correct compound sentence?
A Sentence 1
B Sentence 2
C Sentence 4
D Sentence 6

3. Which sentence has an incorrect joining word?
A Sentence 1
B Sentence 2
C Sentence 5
D Sentence 6

4. Sentence 5 is ___.
A missing a joining word
B not complete
C a simple sentence
D a compound sentence

5. Which word would BEST follow the comma in Sentence 6?
A and
B but
C or
D today

6. Which sentences could be joined with a comma followed by *but*?
A Sentences 1 and 2
B Sentences 3 and 4
C Sentences 4 and 5
D Sentences 5 and 6

Name _____

▲ Rewrite the sentences. Use commas and joining words correctly.

1. My father is a teacher and he works at a school.
   My father is a teacher, and he works at a school.

2. He drives to work, he takes a bus.
   He drives to work, or he takes a bus.

3. He has lunch at work or he eats in the park.
   He has lunch at work, or he eats in the park.

4. Most days he eats tuna, today he eats egg salad.
   Most days he eats tuna, but today he eats egg salad.

▲ Rewrite each pair of sentences as one sentence. Use commas and the joining words *and* or *but* correctly.

5. Mrs. Lopez loves to read. She owns a bookstore.
   Mrs. Lopez loves to read, and she owns a bookstore.

6. The store is small. It has many books.
   The store is small, but it has many books.

7. Sasha works with animals. She enjoys her job.
   Sasha works with animals, and she enjoys her job.

8. She lives in the country. She works in the city.
   She lives in the country, but she works in the city.

Name _____

▲ Underline the common nouns. Circle the proper nouns.

1. (Officer Chan) is from (Dallas), (Texas).
2. (Marta) has a dog named (Rufus).
3. The family adopts two tiny kittens.
4. Fish swim in the (Atlantic Ocean).
5. Kangaroos and koalas live in (Australia).
6. (Steve) visits the big zoo in (Los Angeles).
7. The children see a pretty deer.
8. There are many seals in (Canada) and (Greenland).
9. (Charlie) rides a black horse at the fair.
10. (Mr. Jones) feeds the birds in (Central Park).
11. People watch bats in (Gainesville), (Florida).
12. (Buffy) is a white dog, and (Puff) is an orange cat.

Try This

Find an article in a magazine. List five common nouns from the article. Then list five proper nouns. **Accept reasonable responses.**

Common and Proper Nouns
Lesson 7

Name _____

▲ Rewrite each sentence correctly. Capitalize the proper nouns.

1. A zookeeper came to class on thursday.
   A zookeeper came to class on Thursday.

2. Emma got a rabbit on valentine's day.
   Emma got a rabbit on Valentine's Day.

3. On saturday we visited the animal park.
   On Saturday we visited the animal park.

4. The children learned about the first thanksgiving.
   The children learned about the first Thanksgiving.

5. The first day of winter was wednesday, december 21.
   The first day of winter was Wednesday, December 21.

6. Presidents' day was in february.
   Presidents' Day was in February.

7. Which holiday was on friday, november 11?
   Which holiday was on Friday, November 11?

8. Elijah went to the beach every sunday in july.
   Elijah went to the beach every Sunday in July.

9. The family went on vacation in december.
   The family went on vacation in December.

10. The memorial day picnic was on monday, may 28.
    The Memorial Day picnic was on Monday, May 28.

Grammar–Writing Connection
Lesson 7

Name _____

▲ Read this part of a student's rough draft. Then answer the questions that follow.

(1) Robin and Pam are sisters, and they live in Michigan. (2) Their family got a new puppy on labor day. (3) Daisy is a guide dog, and she will help blind people when she grows up. (4) The children and their parents raise the puppy. (5) Every _____ they go to a dog training class in Detroit.

1. Which word in Sentence 1 is a common noun?
   A Robin
   B sisters
   C live
   D Michigan

2. Which word or words in Sentence 2 should be capitalized?
   A family
   B new
   C puppy
   D labor day

3. Which of these words in Sentence 3 is NOT a noun?
   A Daisy
   B dog
   C grows
   D people

4. How many nouns are in Sentence 4?
   A 1
   B 2
   C 3
   D 4

5. A proper noun belongs in the blank in Sentence 5. Which word is correct?
   A Saturday
   B week
   C Holiday
   D april

6. Which sentence does NOT have a proper noun?
   A Sentence 1
   B Sentence 3
   C Sentence 4
   D Sentence 5

Name _____

▲ Rewrite each sentence correctly.

1. danny has a Partner in the classroom.
   Danny has a partner in the classroom.

2. Her Name is ann.
   Her name is Ann.

3. Danny and ann study every Afternoon.
   Danny and Ann study every afternoon.

4. On fridays the Children learn math.
   On Fridays the children learn math.

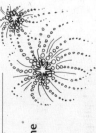

▲ Rewrite each sentence correctly. Underline the common nouns. Circle the proper nouns.

5. Independence day was on tuesday.
   Independence Day was on Tuesday.

6. Yani's class went to new york city and saw fireworks.
   Yani's class went to New York City and saw fireworks.

7. Lights filled the sky over the hudson river.
   Lights filled the sky over the Hudson River.

8. The Students wrote a report about their trip.
   The students wrote a report about their trip.

Name _____

▲ Write the abbreviations for the underlined words.

1. Jean-Luc visits the United States.
   U.S.

2. Springfield is a city in Illinois.
   IL

3. Doctor Witky lives on Pine Road.
   Dr., Rd.

4. Tanisha is from New Mexico, but now she lives in Washington.
   NM, WA

5. The police station is on the corner of East Street and North Avenue.
   St., Ave.

6. Oregon is next to California.
   OR, CA

7. Mistress Rosen owns a house in Rhode Island.
   Mrs., RI

8. Write to Mister Ngo at 122 Long Avenue, Gary, Indiana.
   Mr., Ave., IN

9. Lake Erie is north of Ohio, Pennsylvania, and New York.
   OH, PA, NY

10. Doctor Harrison takes a bus from Mississippi to Alabama.
    Dr., MS, AL

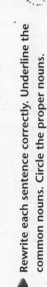

Abbreviations
Lesson 8

▲ **Write the abbreviation for each word.**

1. January
   Jan.

2. Saturday
   Sat.

3. Wednesday
   Wed.

4. March
   Mar.

5. September
   Sept.

6. Friday
   Fri.

▲ **Correct the abbreviations.**

7. Oct 19
   Oct. 19

8. aug. 25
   Aug. 25

9. mon, feb. 5
   Mon., Feb. 5

10. tues, nov 9
    Tues., Nov. 9

Grammar-Writing
Connection
Lesson 8

▲ **Read this part of a student's rough draft. Then answer the questions that follow.**

(1) _____ Block studies the animals in the ocean. (2) He came to our school on Thursday, December 29. (3) Our school is in ME. (4) He drove his car from MA. (5) The students in Mistress Lewis's class enjoyed his talk.

1. Which abbreviation could go in the blank in Sentence 1?
   A Mr
   B mr
   Ⓒ Mr.
   D dr.

2. Which is the correct abbreviation for the underlined word in Sentence 2?
   A thu.
   B TH
   C Thurs
   Ⓓ Thurs.

3. Which is the correct abbreviation for the month in Sentence 2?
   Ⓐ Dec.
   B dec.
   C DE
   D dec

4. Which word should replace the abbreviation in Sentence 3?
   A Massachusetts
   Ⓑ Maine
   C Minnesota
   D Mississippi

5. Which word should replace the abbreviation in Sentence 4?
   Ⓐ Massachusetts
   B Maine
   C Minnesota
   D Montana

6. Which is the correct abbreviation for the underlined word in Sentence 5?
   A Mrs
   Ⓑ Mrs.
   C Ms
   D Ms.

Name _____

▲ Write the full word for each abbreviation.

1. FL   **Florida**

2. Tues.   **Tuesday**

3. Dr.   **Doctor**

4. St.   **Street**

5. Apr.   **April**

▲ Find the words in each sentence that have abbreviations. Write the abbreviations.

6. Mister Ward's party is on Sunday, November 5.
   Mr., Sun., Nov.

7. Send the letter to Doctor Johnson at 5 Mesa Street, El Paso, Texas.
   Dr., St., TX

8. In September, Mistress Torres's class goes to the animal shelter on River Avenue.
   Sept., Mrs., Ave.

9. Tennessee and Missouri are next to Kentucky.
   TN, MO, KY

10. Mistress Brecht spoke at the school on Barstow Road on Friday.
    Mrs., Rd., Fri.

Grammar Practice Book
© Harcourt • Grade 3

© Harcourt • Grade 3

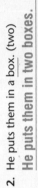
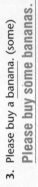

Name _____

▲ Rewrite each sentence using the plural form of the underlined noun. Use the word in parentheses ( ) before each plural noun.

1. Ari bakes a cake. (two)
   Ari bakes two cakes.

2. He puts them in a box. (two)
   He puts them in two boxes.

3. Please buy a banana. (some)
   Please buy some bananas.

4. We need a bunch. (three)
   We need three bunches.

5. Lily picks a berry. (ten)
   Lily picks ten berries.

6. Marco wants a cookie. (four)
   Marco wants four cookies.

7. Abby eats a pear. (two)
   Abby eats two pears.

8. She gives her sister a cherry. (five)
   She gives her sister five cherries.

9. My father cuts a pepper. (two)
   My father cuts two peppers.

10. My brother eats a bite. (three)
    My brother eats three bites.

Grammar Practice Book
© Harcourt • Grade 3

Name _____

▲ Rewrite each sentence using the plural form of the underlined noun. Use a dictionary if you need to. Each new sentence is started for you.

1. One child had cereal for breakfast.
   Three **children had cereal for breakfast.**

2. One woman baked brownies.
   Two **women baked brownies.**

3. One mouse ran to the food bowl.
   Three **mice ran to the food bowl.**

4. One deer pulled leaves from the tree.
   Four **deer pulled leaves from the tree.**

5. One goose ate the bread.
   Five **geese ate the bread.**

▲ Rewrite each sentence. Replace the singular nouns in parentheses ( ) with the plural form. Use a dictionary if you need to.

6. Billy's (foot) are tired.
   Billy's feet are tired.

7. Billy and the (man) cook soup for dinner.
   Billy and the men cook soup for dinner.

8. After dinner he brushes his (tooth).
   After dinner he brushes his teeth.

Name _____

▲ Read this part of a student's rough draft. Then answer the questions that follow.

(1) It is Josh's turn to set the table. (2) He uses his family's best dish. (3) He takes out a fork and spoons. (4) He puts out glasses for the men and women. (5) He puts out cups for the child. (6) Now _____ can be served.

1. Which is the correct plural form of the underlined word in Sentence 2?
   A dishs
   B dishies
   C dishes
   D dish

2. Which is the correct plural form of the underlined word in Sentence 3?
   A forkes
   B forks
   C forkies
   D fork

3. Which word in Sentence 4 is NOT a plural noun?
   A puts
   B glasses
   C men
   D women

4. The underlined word in Sentence 5 should be in its plural form. Which is correct?
   A child
   B childs
   C childes
   D children

5. A singular noun belongs in the blank in Sentence 6. Which word is correct?
   A dinners
   B dineries
   C dinner's
   D dinner

6. Which sentence does NOT have a plural noun?
   A Sentence 1
   B Sentence 3
   C Sentence 4
   D Sentence 5

Name _____

▲ Write the correct plural form of each singular noun. Use a dictionary if you need to.

1. pot   pots
2. raspberry   raspberries
3. tomato   tomatoes
4. meal   meals
5. rabbit   rabbits
6. moose   moose
7. sheep   sheep
8. puppy   puppies

▲ Rewrite the sentences. Use the plural forms of the nouns in parentheses ( ). Use a dictionary if you need to.

9. The (child) made (sandwich).
The children made sandwiches.

10. Amber sliced (carrot) and (apple).
Amber sliced carrots and apples.

11. Do you want (blueberry) or (peach)?
Do you want blueberries or peaches?

12. Brush your (tooth) after you eat the (strawberry).
Brush your teeth after you eat the strawberries.

Name _____

▲ Read this part of a student's rough draft. Then answer the questions that follow.

(1) Mrs. Sanchez's class performed a play on _____, October 2. (2) The Play was at the Madison Elementary School. (3) At 7:00 P.M. (4) My sister Elaine acted, she did a great job. (5) My bedtime is 8:00 P.M. (6) My parents let me stay up late to watch the play.

1. Which word could go in the blank in Sentence 1?
A Monday
B tuesday
C evening
D lunchtime

2. Which word in Sentence 2 is incorrectly capitalized?
A Play
B Madison
C Elementary
D School

3. Which word should follow the comma in Sentence 4?
A but
B or
C and
D tonight

4. Which is the proper noun in Sentence 4?
A sister
B Elaine
C great
D job

5. Which two simple sentences could be joined by a comma followed by *but*?
A Sentences 1 and 2
B Sentences 3 and 4
C Sentences 4 and 5
D Sentences 5 and 6

6. Which sentence is NOT complete?
A Sentence 2
B Sentence 3
C Sentence 5
D Sentence 6

Name _____

▶ **Write the possessive noun in each sentence. Label it as *singular* or *plural*.**

1. Rico's family has three children.
   Rico's; singular

2. My brothers' toys are on the floor.
   brothers'; plural

3. Her sister's name is Kristen.
   sister's; singular

4. Mason rides in his aunt's car.
   aunt's; singular

5. The families' homes are nearby.
   families'; plural

6. The boys' grandfather comes to visit.
   boys'; plural

7. What is your mother's job?
   mother's; singular

8. Shane wears his cousin's hat.
   cousin's; singular

9. Mr. Daly enjoys his sons' softball game.
   sons'; plural

10. The dog's leash is on the table.
    dog's; singular

Name _____

▶ **Read this part of a student's rough draft. Then answer the questions that follow.**

> (1) There is a mystery to solve at 10 Mountain Road. (2) The Brooks children can't find their puppy. (3) What are the clue? (4) The door is open, and cookies are baking in the house across the street. (5) _____ Brooks says she knows where the puppy is. (6) Do you?

1. What is the abbreviation for the underlined word in Sentence 1?
   A rd
   B rd.
   C Rd.
   D RD

2. What is the correct plural form of the noun in Sentence 3?
   A clue
   B clues
   C cluees
   D cluies

3. How many SINGULAR nouns are in Sentence 4?
   A two
   B three
   C four
   D five

4. How many PLURAL nouns are in Sentence 4?
   A one
   B two
   C three
   D four

5. Which abbreviation could go in the blank in Sentence 5?
   A mrs
   B Mrs
   C MS
   D Mrs.

6. Which sentence has an irregular plural noun?
   A Sentence 2
   B Sentence 3
   C Sentence 4
   D Sentence 5

Name _____

▲ If the underlined word needs an apostrophe ('), rewrite it correctly. If it is correct, write *correct*.

1. Ms. Roth held her daughters hand.   **daughter's**

2. The schools auditorium was full.   **school's**

3. The boys performed in a play.   **correct**

4. My fathers camera was broken.   **father's**

5. The student read two poems.   **correct**

6. How many songs did they sing?   **correct**

▲ Write the plural form of each noun. Then write the plural possessive form.

7. uncle   **uncles**   **uncles'**

8. grandson   **grandsons**   **grandsons'**

9. violinist   **violinists**   **violinists'**

10. glass   **glasses**   **glasses'**

11. cherry   **cherries**   **cherries'**

12. banana   **bananas**   **bananas'**

Name _____

▲ Read this part of a student's rough draft. Then answer the questions that follow.

(1) Mr. Kwon class put on a show. (2) The students families were in the audience. (3) The student's performed different acts. (4) The act of Rachel was funny. (5) Rachel's parents smiled and clapped. (6) All the parents enjoyed the show.

1. Which singular possessive noun should be a plural noun?
A show (Sentence 1)
B audience (Sentence 2)
C student's (Sentence 3)
D act (Sentence 4)

2. Which singular noun should also be possessive?
A Mr. Kwon (Sentence 1)
B audience (Sentence 2)
C act (Sentence 4)
D show (Sentence 6)

3. Which plural noun should also be possessive?
A students (Sentence 2)
B families (Sentence 2)
C acts (Sentence 3)
D parents (Sentence 5)

4. How could you rewrite the underlined phrase in Sentence 4?
A the act's of Rachel
B the acts of Rachel
C Rachel's act
D Rachels' act

5. Which other word could replace *parents* in Sentence 6?
A parents'
B families'
C students'
D families

6. Which sentence is correct as it is written?
A Sentence 1
B Sentence 2
C Sentence 3
D Sentence 5

Name _____

Possessive Nouns
Lesson 11

▲ Rewrite each phrase. Use the correct possessive noun.

1. the costumes that belong to the girls
   the girls' costumes

2. the dance of Ron
   Ron's dance

3. the necklace owned by her grandmother
   her grandmother's necklace

4. the bottles of the babies
   the babies' bottles

5. the sleeves of the dresses
   the dresses' sleeves

6. the car that belongs to my mother
   my mother's car

▲ Write sentences using the noun below. The words in parentheses ( ) tell which form of the noun to use. **Possible responses are shown.**

dancer

7. (singular) **A dancer performed at school.**

8. (plural) **Two dancers are on stage.**

9. (singular possessive) **The dancer's costume is pretty.**

10. (plural possessive) **The dancers' legs were sore.**

Grammar Practice Book
© Harcourt • Grade 3

Name _____

Singular and Plural Pronouns
Lesson 12

▲ Write the two singular pronouns in each sentence.

1. She sent me a postcard.
   She, me

2. Where did he put it?
   he, it

3. I gave her the box.
   I, her

4. It was a gift for you.
   It, you

5. You spoke to him today.
   You, him

6. He saw you yesterday.
   He, you

7. She told me the story.
   She, me

8. I enjoyed reading it.
   I, it

9. You wrote a letter to her.
   You, her

10. Did it interest him?
    it, him

Grammar Practice Book
© Harcourt • Grade 3

Student Edition pp. 40–41

Name _____

▲ Write the plural pronoun in each sentence.

1. We took a flight to Mexico. __We__

2. My aunt and uncle met us at the airport. __us__

3. They smiled and said "Welcome!" __They__

4. My sister was excited to see them. __them__

▲ Rewrite each sentence. Use a plural pronoun to replace each underlined phrase.

5. The girls went to camp last summer.
   They went to camp last summer.

6. The girls wrote to my friend and me.
   The girls wrote to us.

7. My friend and I wrote to the girls.
   We wrote to the girls.

8. My friend and I told the girls about our soccer team.
   My friend and I told them about our soccer team.

9. Did you and your brother send letters to the girls?
   Did you send letters to the girls?

10. The girls were happy to get the letters.
    The girls were happy to get them.

11. The letters arrived every Monday.
    They arrived every Monday.

12. They just got a letter from Mom and Dad.
    They just got a letter from them.

Name _____

▲ Read this part of a student's rough draft. Then answer the questions that follow.

> (1) Natasha has a pen pal named Chen. (2) Chen lives in China. (3) Natasha and Chen write every week. (4) Natasha and Chen tell each other about the things they do. (5) Last week Natasha wrote to Chen about the school play. (6) Natasha told him that everyone enjoyed the play.

1. Which sentence has a singular pronoun?
   A Sentence 1
   B Sentence 3
   C Sentence 4
   (D) Sentence 6

2. Which sentence has a plural pronoun?
   A Sentence 1
   B Sentence 3
   (C) Sentence 4
   D Sentence 6

3. Which pronoun could replace the underlined word in Sentence 2?
   (A) He
   B Him
   C They
   D It

4. Which pronoun could replace the underlined words in Sentence 4?
   A He
   B She
   (C) They
   D Them

5. Which pronoun could replace the underlined word in Sentence 6?
   A It
   (B) She
   C Her
   D They

6. Which word(s) could be replaced by the pronoun it?
   A Natasha (Sentence 1)
   B Natasha and Chen (Sentence 3)
   C week (Sentence 5)
   (D) the play (Sentence 6)

Singular and Plural Pronouns — Lesson 12

Name _____

▲ Write the pronoun in each sentence. Then label each as *S* (singular) or *P* (plural).

1. We learned about Chile today. __We; P__

2. Mr. Edwards showed us two maps. __us; P__

3. He hung the maps on the wall. __He; S__

4. They showed volcanoes and a desert. __They; P__

5. The students looked at them carefully. __them; P__

6. Mr. Edwards asked me to point to the desert. __me; S__

▲ Rewrite each sentence with a correct pronoun. **Possible responses are shown.**

7. Ellen studied Spanish because _____ wanted to visit Spain.
Ellen studied Spanish because she wanted to visit Spain.

8. The class was fun, and the students enjoyed _____.
The class was fun, and the students enjoyed it.

9. The teacher brought pictures to show _____.
The teacher brought pictures to shown them.

10. He took the pictures when _____ was in Spain.
He took the pictures when he was in Spain.

Subject and Object Pronouns — Lesson 13

Name _____

▲ Write the pronoun in each sentence. Then label each pronoun as *subject* or *object*.

1. Ms. Edison teaches us about flowers.
__us; object__

2. A student asks her how flowers grow.
__her; object__

3. Ms. Edison answers him.
__him; object__

4. She talks to the class about sunlight.
__She; subject__

5. Flowers need it to make food and grow.
__it; object__

6. We learn more about flowers.
__We; subject__

7. Bees collect pollen from them.
__them; object__

8. I write a paper on flowers.
__I; subject__

Try This

Find four sentences in a book or magazine that have pronouns. Copy the sentences. Underline the subject pronouns. Circle the object pronouns. **Accept reasonable responses.**

Subject and
Object Pronouns
Lesson 13

▲ Rewrite each sentence. Use subject pronouns correctly.

1. Me and Anna went to the library.
   Anna and I went to the library.

2. I and she studied trees.
   She and I studied trees.

3. You and me looked at books and pictures.
   You and I looked at books and pictures.

4. Me and he learned about pine trees.
   He and I learned about pine trees.

5. I and Deon wrote a report together.
   Deon and I wrote a report together.

▲ Rewrite each sentence. Use object pronouns correctly.

6. Show the flowers to Ryan and I.
   Show the flowers to Ryan and me.

7. My mother gave me and my sister a plant.
   My mother gave my sister and me a plant.

8. Please help him and I with the report.
   Please help him and me with the report.

9. Jenny came to the library with him and I.
   Jenny came to the library with him and me.

10. The librarian offered to help me and Ryan.
    The librarian offered to help Ryan and me.

Grammar Practice Book
© Harcourt • Grade 3

Student Edition pp. 46–47

Grammar–Writing
Connection
Lesson 13

▲ Read this part of a student's rough draft. Then answer the questions that follow.

(1) Me and my mother planted an apple seed in a pot. (2) We watered the seed. (3) The seed grew leaves and roots. (4) My mother moved it to the yard. (5) I watched my mother pack soil around the little plant. (6) One day the seed will become an apple tree.

1. Which sentence has a singular subject pronoun?
   A Sentence 2
   B Sentence 3
   C Sentence 4
   D Sentence 5

2. Which sentence has a plural subject pronoun?
   A Sentence 2
   B Sentence 4
   C Sentence 5
   D Sentence 6

3. Which type of pronoun is *it* in Sentence 4?
   A a singular subject pronoun
   B plural subject pronoun
   C singular object pronoun
   D plural object pronoun

4. How should the underlined phrase in Sentence 1 be written?
   A My mother and me
   B Me and her
   C Her and me
   D My mother and I

5. Which of these could replace the underlined words in Sentence 3?
   A a singular subject pronoun
   B a plural subject pronoun
   C a singular object pronoun
   D a plural object pronoun

6. Which of these could replace the underlined words in Sentence 5?
   A a singular subject pronoun
   B a plural subject pronoun
   C a singular object pronoun
   D a plural object pronoun

Grammar Practice Book
© Harcourt • Grade 3

Subject and Object Pronouns — Lesson 13

Name _____

▲ Write a subject or object pronoun to replace each underlined word or phrase.

1. Ariel's sister taught Ariel about bees. **her**

2. Ariel's sister told Ariel that bees are insects. **She**

3. Ariel and I watched bees in the park. **We**

4. Ariel and I saw the bees fly. **them**

5. Ariel's father gave Ariel and me a book. **us**

6. The book had pictures of bees. **It**

▲ Rewrite each sentence. Use *I* and *me* correctly.

7. You and me picked pears from the tree.
You and I picked pears from the tree.

8. Todd ate cherries with my friend and I.
Todd ate cherries with my friend and me.

9. Me and my brother sliced apples.
My brother and I sliced apples.

10. They shared the plums with me and him.
They shared the plums with him and me.

Pronoun–Antecedent Agreement — Lesson 14

Name _____

▲ Write the correct pronoun for each sentence. Then write the noun that it refers to.

1. A bird catches worms and brings (it/them) back to the nest.
them, worms

2. A mouse eats the crumbs that (it/they) finds.
it, mouse

3. The dogs see the man, and (him/they) start to bark.
they, dogs

4. John sees Michael and waves to (him/them).
him, Michael

5. Squirrels gather nuts and hide (it/them).
them, nuts

6. A spider spins a web and traps flies in (it/them).
it, web

7. Bats eat the insects that (it/they) catch.
they, bats

8. Simon sees two little kittens and stops to pet (him/them).
them, kittens

9. A bear goes into a cave, where (it/they) sleeps all winter.
it, bear

10. The boys buy a gift for Mrs. Johnson and give it to (her/them).
her, Mrs. Johnson

Name _____

▲ Rewrite each sentence. Replace the underlined word or phrase with a pronoun.

1. Luis hugs Beth and welcomes Beth home.
   Luis hugs Beth and welcomes her home.

2. Beth smiles at Luis and thanks Luis.
   Beth smiles at Luis and thanks him.

3. My sister invites Beth to play in the garden.
   She invites Beth to play in the garden.

4. Luis goes to the garden too, and Luis plants flowers.
   Luis goes to the garden too, and he plants flowers.

5. Beth finds an anthill when Beth is in the yard.
   Beth finds an anthill when she is in the yard.

6. John makes dinner while John is in the kitchen.
   John makes dinner while he is in the kitchen.

7. He bakes cookies for Janet and gives them to Janet.
   He bakes cookies for Janet and gives them to her.

8. Janet eats a cookie, and Janet thanks John.
   Janet eats a cookie, and she thanks John.

9. John is pleased because John loves to bake.
   John is pleased because he loves to bake.

10. Janet buys John a cookbook and gives the cookbook to him.
    Janet buys John a cookbook and gives it to him.

Name _____

▲ Read this part of a student's rough draft. Then answer the questions that follow.

(1) Mr. Kay lives in a house that Mr. Kay built. (2) The house is high up in the hills, and it is far from the city. (3) Mr. Kay likes the hills because the hills have a great view of the city. (4) Mr. Kay's children drive up a winding road when she come to visit. (5) The children love their father and enjoy visiting _____

1. Which pronoun could replace the underlined words in Sentence 1?
   (A) he
   B she
   C they
   D it

2. Which pronoun could replace the underlined words in Sentence 3?
   A he
   B she
   (C) they
   D it

3. Which pronoun could go in the blank in Sentence 5?
   A it
   B them
   (C) him
   D her

4. Which word does the pronoun *it* refer to in Sentence 2?
   (A) house
   B high
   C hills
   D city

5. Which sentence has a pronoun that does not agree with the noun it refers to?
   A Sentence 1
   B Sentence 2
   C Sentence 3
   (D) Sentence 4

6. Which pronoun could replace the underlined words in Sentence 5?
   A It
   B Them
   (C) They
   D He

Name _____

Pronoun–
Antecedent
Agreement
Lesson 14

▲ Circle the pronoun in each sentence. Rewrite the sentence. Correct the pronoun so that it agrees with the underlined word.

1. The nest was too high for Maria to see (him).

   The nest was too high for Maria to see it.

2. Maria was excited because (he) saw an owl.

   Maria was excited because she saw an owl.

3. Luke was homesick when (it) went to camp.

   Luke was homesick when he went to camp.

4. The girls invited Hillary to play with (her).

   The girls invited Hillary to play with them.

5. John wrote a letter and sent (them) home.

   John wrote a letter and sent it home.

6. John's parents wrote back to (it).

   John's parents wrote back to him.

▲ Fill in each blank with a correct pronoun. Then underline the word or words that the pronoun refers to.

7. Honeybees live in hives, where ___they___ have jobs to do.

8. Worker bees feed the queen bee and protect ___her___.

9. Honeybees gather nectar and use ___it___ to make honey.

10. Some people keep bees and collect honey from ___them___.

52

Grammar–Writing
Connection
Lesson 15

Name _____

▲ Read this part of a student's rough draft. Then answer the questions that follow.

(1) Tony is the friend of Joan. (2) Tony tells Joan that he is upset. (3) Joan asks he what is wrong. (4) Tony says that he lost his mothers pen. (5) Joan helps him look for the pen. (6) Together they find it under Tony's bed.

1. Which sentence has a singular possessive noun?
   A Sentence 2
   B Sentence 3
   C Sentence 5
   D Sentence 6

2. Which sentence has an incorrectly written possessive noun?
   A Sentence 2
   B Sentence 3
   C Sentence 4
   D Sentence 6

3. Which phrase could replace the underlined phrase in Sentence 1?
   A the friend's of Joan
   B the friends of Joan
   C Joan's friend
   D Joans' friend

4. Which pronoun could replace the underlined word in Sentence 2?
   A he
   B she
   C him
   D her

5. Which pronoun could replace the underlined phrase in Sentence 5?
   A it
   B her
   C him
   D them

6. Which sentence has an incorrect pronoun?
   A Sentence 3
   B Sentence 4
   C Sentence 5
   D Sentence 6

53

29

Grammar–Writing Connection
Lesson 15

▲ **Read this part of a student's rough draft.**
Then answer the questions that follow.

(1) Yasmin writes for a newspaper that she started. (2) She reports on what is new in school. (3) Yesterday Yasmin wrote about something that happened to her. (4) She found a kitten in the school playground. (5) Yasmin took the kitten home and gave them to her father. (6) Her father was happy to have the kitten.

1. Which word does the pronoun in Sentence 1 refer to?
   - A Yasmin
   - B writes
   - C newspaper
   - D she

2. Which sentence has a singular subject pronoun?
   - A Sentence 2
   - B Sentence 3
   - C Sentence 5
   - D Sentence 6

3. Which sentence has a singular object pronoun?
   - A Sentence 2
   - B Sentence 3
   - C Sentence 4
   - D Sentence 6

4. Which sentence has a pronoun that does not agree with the noun that it refers to?
   - A Sentence 1
   - B Sentence 2
   - C Sentence 3
   - D Sentence 5

5. Which could replace the underlined words in Sentence 6?
   - A a singular subject pronoun
   - B a plural subject pronoun
   - C a singular object pronoun
   - D a plural object pronoun

6. Which pronoun could replace the words *the kitten* in Sentence 5?
   - A she
   - B it
   - C they
   - D them

Adjectives
Lesson 16

▲ **Write the adjective. Then write the noun that it describes.**

1. A brown bear sat in the cave. _____ brown, bear

2. The bear was hungry. _____ hungry, bear

3. The forest was big. _____ big, forest

4. The raccoon saw the purple berries. _____ purple, berries

5. The happy raccoon ate the berries. _____ happy, raccoon

6. A small child climbed a rock. _____ small, child

7. The rock was huge. _____ huge, rock

8. A plant grew in a tiny pot. _____ tiny, pot

9. The plant was green. _____ green, plant

10. The pot was round. _____ round, pot

11. The wolf ran through the dark woods. _____ dark, woods

12. The wolf was gray. _____ gray, wolf

Try This

Write two sentences that could begin a story. Use at least one adjective in each sentence. Circle each adjective, and draw an arrow to the noun it describes. **Accept reasonable responses.**

Name _____

▲ Write the adjective that tells how many.

1. Some wolves live in the forest. **Some**

2. Seven wolves run in the pack. **Seven**

3. The wolf has five toes on each paw. **five**

4. A wolf's coat has two layers. **two**

5. Wolves howl for several reasons. **several**

6. The mother wolf has six babies. **six**

▲ Write the adjective that tells how many. Rewrite the sentence.
Replace the number word with an adjective that tells how many
without giving an exact number. **Possible responses are shown.**

7. Four students wrote a story together.
four; A few students wrote a story together.

8. The story was about six squirrels.
six; The story was about some squirrels.

9. A woman read eleven stories to her children.
eleven; A woman read many stories to her children.

10. There were seven pictures in the book.
seven; There were several pictures in the book.

11. The book had ninety pages.
ninety; The book had many pages.

12. Three women waited for the bus to arrive.
Three; A few women waited for the bus to arrive.

Grammar Practice Book
© Harcourt • Grade 3

Name _____

▲ Read this part of a student's rough draft.
Then answer the questions that follow.

> (1) I climbed a little tree in my friend's yard. (2) I picked cherries
> from the tree. (3) I gave _____ cherries to my father. (4) My
> father had green apples at home. (5) He made a beautiful salad with
> the red cherries and two green apples.

1. Which sentence has an
adjective that tells how many?

A Sentence 1
B Sentence 2
C Sentence 4
Ⓓ Sentence 5

2. Which sentence has an
adjective that tells what color?

A Sentence 1
B Sentence 2
C Sentence 3
Ⓓ Sentence 4

3. Which sentence has an
adjective that tells what size?

Ⓐ Sentence 1
B Sentence 2
C Sentence 4
D Sentence 5

4. Which sentence does NOT
have an adjective?

A Sentence 1
Ⓑ Sentence 2
C Sentence 4
D Sentence 5

5. Which is the BEST word to
complete Sentence 3?

A thin
Ⓑ some
C unkind
D big

6. Which sentence has the most
adjectives?

Ⓐ Sentence 1
B Sentence 2
C Sentence 4
Ⓓ Sentence 5

Grammar Practice Book
© Harcourt • Grade 3

Student Edition pp. 56–57

Lesson 16 — Adjectives

Name _____

▲ Underline the two adjectives in each sentence. Then write whether each adjective tells *what kind* or *how many.*

1. Many wolves eat five pounds of food a day.
   how many; how many

2. A few wolves have blue eyes.
   how many; what kind

3. The coats of some wolves are white.
   how many; what kind

4. Big wolves weigh more than ninety pounds.
   what kind; how many

▲ Rewrite the sentences. Add an adjective before each underlined noun. Use an adjective that answers the question in parentheses ( ).
Possible responses are shown.

5. The apple fell from the tree. (What color?)
   The red apple fell from the tree.

6. There were apples on the tree. (How many?)
   There were many apples on the tree.

7. Fatima ate the apple. (What size?)
   Fatima ate the big apple.

8. I cut the apple into slices. (What shape?)
   I cut the round apple into slices.

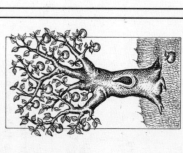

58

Grammar Practice Book
© Harcourt • Grade 3

Adjectives That Compare — Lesson 17

Name _____

▲ Rewrite each sentence. Use the correct form of the adjective in parentheses ( ).

1. The lion is (large) than the fox.
   The lion is larger than the fox.

2. The peacock has the (pretty) feathers of all the birds.
   The peacock has the prettiest feathers of all the birds.

3. The bear is the (strong) animal in the forest.
   The bear is the strongest animal in the forest.

4. The beetle is (tiny) than the worm.
   The beetle is tinier than the worm.

5. The horse runs (fast) than the donkey.
   The horse runs faster than the donkey.

6. That dog has the (loud) bark in town.
   That dog has the loudest bark in town.

7. Sabrina's rabbit is (fluffy) than my rabbit.
   Sabrina's rabbit is fluffier than my rabbit.

8. The dolphin is the (smart) of all the ocean animals.
   The dolphin is the smartest of all the ocean animals.

9. The cat is (friendly) today than it was yesterday.
   The cat is friendlier today than it was yesterday.

10. We have the (cute) pet on the block.
    We have the cutest pet on the block.

59

Grammar Practice Book
© Harcourt • Grade 3

Name _____

▲ Rewrite each sentence. Use *more* or *the most* correctly before each adjective.

1. These berries are _____ delicious than those berries.

   These berries are more delicious than those berries.

2. The cherry tree is _____ beautiful of the three trees.

   The cherry tree is the most beautiful of the three trees.

3. This hike is _____ difficult than the last hike.

   This hike is more difficult than the last hike.

4. A hurricane is _____ frightening than a rainstorm.

   A hurricane is more frightening than a rainstorm.

5. Thunder makes _____ terrifying sound of all.

   Thunder makes the most terrifying sound of all.

6. This is _____ wonderful sunrise that I have ever seen.

   This is the most wonderful sunrise that I have ever seen.

7. The hawk is _____ powerful bird in the forest.

   The hawk is the most powerful bird in the forest.

8. This lake has _____ unusual fish in the state.

   This lake has the most unusual fish in the state.

9. This forest is _____ enormous than the Black Hills National Forest.

   This forest is more enormous than the Black Hills National Forest.

10. This story is _____ interesting one I have ever read.

    This story is the most interesting one I have ever read.

Grammar Practice Book
© Harcourt • Grade 3

Name _____

▲ Read this part of a student's rough draft. Then answer the questions that follow.

> (1) My brother is older than I am. (2) He took me camping in a big forest last weekend. (3) The forest was the beautiful place that I have ever visited. (4) The trees were tall than my house. (5) In the morning we saw a brown bear. (6) I was scared than my brother, and my scream was _____ than his!

1. Which sentence has the correct form of an adjective that compares?
   Ⓐ Sentence 1
   B Sentence 2
   C Sentence 3
   D Sentence 4

2. Which adjective needs the ending -*er*?
   A beautiful (Sentence 3)
   Ⓑ tall (Sentence 4)
   C brown (Sentence 5)
   D scared (Sentence 6)

3. Which adjective needs the word *more* before it?
   A older (Sentence 1)
   B big (Sentence 2)
   C beautiful (Sentence 3)
   Ⓓ scared (Sentence 6)

4. Which adjective needs the word *most* before it?
   A older (Sentence 1)
   Ⓑ beautiful (Sentence 3)
   C brown (Sentence 5)
   D scared (Sentence 6)

5. Which are the correct adjectives that compare for the adjective *big* in Sentence 2?
   Ⓐ bigger, biggest
   B big, biggest
   C more big, most big
   D more bigger, most biggest

6. Which is the BEST way to complete Sentence 6?
   A more loud
   B most loud
   Ⓒ louder
   D loudest

Grammar Practice Book
© Harcourt • Grade 3

Student Edition pp. 60–61

▲ Write the form of each adjective that compares two things. Then write the form that compares three or more things.

1. playful   more playful, most playful

2. funny   funnier, funniest

3. afraid   more afraid, most afraid

4. important   more important, most important

5. high   higher, highest

6. exciting   more exciting, most exciting

▲ Rewrite each sentence correctly.

7. The raccoon was small than the fox.
   The raccoon was smaller than the fox.

8. Today's sunset was lovely than yesterday's sunset.
   Today's sunset was lovelier than yesterday's sunset.

9. That cliff was the most steep one I have ever climbed.
   That cliff was the steepest one I have ever climbed.

10. The river was more deeper than the stream.
   The river was deeper than the stream.

Grammar Practice Book
© Harcourt • Grade 3

▲ Write the article in each sentence and the noun it introduces.

1. Angela went to the city.   the city

2. She visited a friend.   a friend

3. Angela's friend lived in an apartment.   an apartment

4. They took the bus.   the bus

5. They went to a museum.   a museum

6. They saw a painting.   a painting

7. It had a frame.   a frame

8. Children played in the grass.   the grass

9. A bird ate pieces of bread.   A bird

10. The man played his violin.   The man

11. The friends went home.   The friends

12. They took a train.   a train

Try This

Find four sentences that use articles in a book or a magazine. Copy the sentences. Circle the articles. Draw an arrow from each article to the noun it introduces.   Accept reasonable responses.

Grammar Practice Book
© Harcourt • Grade 3

Name _____

▶ **Rewrite each sentence. Use *a* or *an* to fill in the blank.**

1. Jessie's older sister is _____ artist.

   Jessie's older sister is an artist.

2. She is making _____ clay sculpture.

   She is making a clay sculpture.

3. Jeff buys paper and _____ box of paints.

   Jeff buys paper and a box of paints.

4. He draws some squares and _____ oval.

   He draws some squares and an oval.

▶ **Rewrite each sentence. Use *a*, *an*, or *the* to fill in the blank.**

5. Several paintings hang on _____ white walls.

   Several paintings hang on the white walls.

6. Abe is _____ excellent painter.

   Abe is an excellent painter.

7. This is _____ biggest museum.

   This is the biggest museum.

8. You need some paper and _____ pencil for drawing.

   You need some paper and a pencil for drawing.

9. _____ young artists will have an art show.

   The young artists will have an art show.

Name _____

▲ **Read this part of a student's rough draft. Then answer the questions that follow.**

(1) My aunt lives in _____ house in the country. I visited her last weekend. (2) On Saturday we saw a owl. (3) _____ owl was in a tree. (4) On Sunday we rode a tractor and picked apples. (5) My aunt made baked apples that night. (6) _____ apples were delicious.

1. Which of these sentences has an article that is used correctly?
   A Sentence 2
   (B) Sentence 4
   C Sentence 5
   D Sentence 6

2. In which sentence should the article *a* be changed to *an*?
   (A) Sentence 2
   B Sentence 3
   C Sentence 4
   D Sentence 6

3. Which word should fill in the blank in Sentence 6?
   A A
   B An
   (C) The
   D One

4. Which word would BEST fill in the blank in Sentence 1?
   (A) a
   B an
   C the
   D several

5. Which word would BEST fill in the blank in Sentence 3?
   A A
   B An
   (C) The
   D Some

6. Which sentence does NOT have an article?
   A Sentence 1
   B Sentence 3
   C Sentence 4
   (D) Sentence 5

Name _____

▲ Use the articles *a*, *an*, and *the* to write two singular forms of each plural noun.

Examples: birds: a bird, the bird
              icy roads: an icy road, the icy road

1. skyscrapers   a skyscraper, the skyscraper
2. elevators   an elevator, the elevator
3. rooftops   a rooftop, the rooftop
4. noisy trains a noisy train, the noisy train
5. escalators   an escalator, the escalator
6. shops   a shop, the shop
7. airports   an airport, the airport
8. excited boys an excited boy, the excited boy
9. red cars   a red car, the red car

▲ Write a sentence for each article. Circle the article, and underline the noun that it introduces. Possible responses are shown.

10. a   (A) boy walked his dog.
11. an   I saw (an) elephant.
12. the It's fun to visit (the) big city.

Grammar Practice Book
© Harcourt • Grade 3

Name _____

▲ Write the complete predicate of each sentence. Underline the action verb.

1. The woman walks to the market.
   walks to the market

2. She buys fruit and vegetables.
   buys fruit and vegetables

3. The animals gather in the yard.
   gather in the yard

4. The cows moo at the ducks.
   moo at the ducks

5. The sun shines brightly.
   shines brightly

6. The weather reporter predicts rain.
   predicts rain

7. The boy helps his sister.
   helps his sister

8. The children eat a good meal.
   eat a good meal

9. I enjoy the folktale.
   enjoy the folktale

10. We discuss the characters.
    discuss the characters

Grammar Practice Book
© Harcourt • Grade 3

Name _____

Action Verbs
Lesson 19

▲ **Underline the correct action verb in each sentence.**

1. The chicken (lay/<u>lays</u>) five eggs.

2. Ava (watch/<u>watches</u>) the little chicks.

3. I (<u>plant</u>/plants) corn and tomatoes.

4. He (<u>plow</u>/plows) the field.

5. Children (<u>play</u>/plays) near the barn.

6. We (<u>sell</u>/sells) milk and cheese.

7. The dog (bark/<u>barks</u>) loudly.

▲ **Choose an action verb from the box to complete each sentence. Then write the sentence.**

takes	carry	wakes	scratch	scatters

8. The chickens _____ in the dirt.
   The chickens scratch in the dirt.

9. The rooster _____ everyone.
   The rooster wakes everyone.

10. We _____ a basket of eggs.
    We carry a basket of eggs.

11. Tyrell _____ eggs to the market.
    Tyrell takes eggs to the market.

12. She _____ feed around the yard.
    She scatters feed around the yard.

Name _____

Grammar–Writing
Connection
Lesson 19

▶ **Read this part of a student's rough draft. Then answer the questions that follow.**

(1) Rosa lives in Mexico City. (2) She _____ soccer. (3) She and her father watch games together on TV. (4) One Sunday they ride a bus to a game at a stadium. (5) The home team wins. (6) The excited fans stand and cheer.

1. Which is the verb in Sentence 1?
   A Rosa
   B lives
   C in
   D Mexico

2. Which of these action verbs does not agree with its subject?
   A watch (Sentence 3)
   B rides (Sentence 4)
   C wins (Sentence 5)
   D stand (Sentence 6)

3. Which sentence has a singular subject and a verb that agrees?
   A Sentence 2
   B Sentence 3
   C Sentence 5
   D Sentence 6

4. Which action verb could complete Sentence 2?
   A like
   B enjoy
   C loves
   D play

5. Which sentence has two action verbs?
   A Sentence 3
   B Sentence 4
   C Sentence 5
   D Sentence 6

6. Which sentence has a plural subject and a verb that agrees?
   A Sentence 1
   B Sentence 3
   C Sentence 4
   D Sentence 5

Name _____

▲ Rewrite each sentence. Use the correct form of the verb in parentheses ( ).

1. An egg (hatch/hatches) in the nest.
   An egg hatches in the nest.

2. The ducklings (follow/follows) their mother.
   The ducklings follow their mother.

3. The farmer (hurry/hurries) home.
   The farmer hurries home.

4. Mice (scurry/scurries) around the barn.
   Mice scurry around the barn.

5. We (milk/milks) the cows every morning.
   We milk the cows every morning.

6. She (drive/drives) the big tractor.
   She drives the big tractor.

7. Jessica (help/helps) my brother dry dishes.
   Jessica helps my brother dry dishes.

8. They (clean/cleans) the kitchen.
   They clean the kitchen.

70

Grammar Practice Book
© Harcourt • Grade 3

Name _____

▲ Read this part of a student's rough draft. Then answer the questions that follow.

(1) There was an art show at the library yesterday. (2) Children displayed their art. (3) I showed two paintings. (4) They were the largest ones in the room. (5) There were also _____ photographs and a black sculpture. (6) The sculpture was interesting than the photographs.

1. Which sentence uses the correct form of an adjective that compares?
   A Sentence 3
   B Sentence 4
   C Sentence 5
   D Sentence 6

2. Which adjective needs the word *more* before it?
   A two (Sentence 3)
   B largest (Sentence 4)
   C black (Sentence 5)
   D interesting (Sentence 6)

3. Which adjective could be written before *Children* in Sentence 2?
   A Many
   B One
   C Hundred
   D Each

4. Which adjective that tells *what kind* could fill in the blank in Sentence 5?
   A biggest
   B tiniest
   C small
   D some

5. Which sentence has an adjective that tells *what color?*
   A Sentence 1
   B Sentence 3
   C Sentence 4
   D Sentence 5

6. Which of these sentences does NOT have an adjective?
   A Sentence 2
   B Sentence 3
   C Sentence 4
   D Sentence 5

71

Grammar Practice Book
© Harcourt • Grade 3

© Harcourt • Grade 3

Student Edition pp. 70–71

Name _____

▲ **Write the form of the verb *be* in each sentence.**

1. Laura is cold without her hat. __is__

2. The winter was long. __was__

3. The gloves are on the chair. __are__

4. I am warmer now. __am__

5. The girls were at home. __were__

6. Julio is with Laura. __is__

7. The children are at the skating rink. __are__

8. Those boys were good skaters. __were__

9. The lake is frozen this morning. __is__

10. The grass is covered with snow. __is__

11. I am tired at the end of the day. __am__

12. A huge snowball is next to the house. __is__

13. It is the beginning of a snowman. __is__

14. We were excited to begin. __were__

15. I am freezing outside. __am__

Try This

Write four sentences about your classroom, using the verb *be*. Use a singular subject in two sentences and a plural subject in the other two. Underline the forms of the verb *be*. **Accept reasonable responses.**

Name _____

▲ **Read this part of a student's rough draft. Then answer the questions that follow.**

(1) Luke interviews his mother for a newsletter at school. (2) He asks his mother questions and writes down a answers. (3) questions are about his mother's job. (4) Luke's mother is a engineer. (5) She plans bridges, and people builds them. (6) Students enjoy the report that Luke writes.

1. In which sentence should the article be changed to *an*?

A Sentence 1
B Sentence 2
C Sentence 4
D Sentence 6

2. Which word could fill in the blank in Sentence 3?

A A
B An
C The
D Writes

3. Which sentence has a plural noun with an article that does NOT agree?

A Sentence 1
B Sentence 2
C Sentence 4
D Sentence 6

4. Which of these action verbs does NOT agree with its subject?

A interviews (Sentence 1)
B writes (Sentence 2)
C plans (Sentence 5)
D builds (Sentence 5)

5. Which sentence has only one action verb?

A Sentence 1
B Sentence 2
C Sentence 5
D Sentence 6

6. Which sentence has a plural subject and an action verb that agrees?

A Sentence 1
B Sentence 2
C Sentence 4
D Sentence 6

Student Edition pp. 72–73

The Verb *Be*
Lesson 21

▲ Rewrite each sentence. Choose the correct form of the verb *be* in parentheses ( ).

1. It (is, are) summer.
   It is summer.

2. I (is, am) at the ocean.
   I am at the ocean.

3. We (was, were) warm in the sun.
   We were warm in the sun.

4. He (is, am) in the water.
   He is in the water.

5. They (was, were) with their friends.
   They were with their friends.

6. You (is, are) on a beach blanket.
   You are on a beach blanket.

7. I (was, are) at the snack bar.
   I was at the snack bar.

8. It (is, are) next to a playground.
   It is next to a playground.

9. They (is, are) on the swings.
   They are on the swings.

10. She (is, are) sleepy at the end of the day.
    She is sleepy at the end of the day.

Grammar-Writing Connection
Lesson 21

▲ Read this part of a student's rough draft. Then answer the questions that follow.

(1) My friends and I are at a park. (2) We is very happy. (3) Flowers are everywhere. (4) A squirrel _____ in a tree. (5) I smile at it. (6) Spring are my favorite season.

1. Which sentence has a form of the verb *be* that does NOT agree with the subject?
   A Sentence 1
   B Sentence 2
   C Sentence 3
   D Sentence 5

2. Which does NOT have a form of the verb *be?*
   A Sentence 1
   B Sentence 3
   C Sentence 5
   D Sentence 6

3. Which could go in the blank in Sentence 4?
   A am
   B is
   C are
   D were

4. How should the form of the verb *be* in Sentence 6 be written?
   A am
   B are
   C were
   D is

5. Which has a form of the verb *be* that links the subject to words that tell *what?*
   A Sentence 1
   B Sentence 3
   C Sentence 5
   D Sentence 6

6. Which has a form of the verb *be* that links the subject to words that tell *where?*
   A Sentence 1
   B Sentence 2
   C Sentence 5
   D Sentence 6

Name _____

The Verb *Be*
Lesson 21

▲ Circle the form of the verb *be* in each sentence. Then write whether each links the subject to words that tell *what* or *where*.

1. Some seals (are) white. _____ what

2. The penguin chick (was) fuzzy. _____ what

3. You (were) on the shore. _____ where

4. That shark (is) near a whale. _____ where

5. I (am) with my parents. _____ where

6. They (are) scientists. _____ what

▲ Rewrite each sentence, using a correct form of the verb *be*. Then write *S* above each singular subject and *P* above each plural subject.
Possible responses are shown.

7. Those fish _____ small and silver.
       P
   Those fish are small and silver.

8. We _____ close to the beaver's dam.
   P
   We were close to the beaver's dam.

9. He _____ in a wooden boat.
   S
   He was in a wooden boat.

10. The river _____ full of life.
    S
    The river is full of life.

Name _____

Main and
Helping Verbs
Lesson 22

▲ Circle the helping verb and underline the main verb in each sentence.

1. Some butterflies (can) fly long distances.

2. Moths (are) attracted to the light.

3. The mosquito (could) bite you!

4. We (have) seen many insects this summer.

5. She (will) study bees at the library.

6. I (am) writing a report on ladybugs.

7. The bats (were) looking for food.

8. You (should) watch that hummingbird.

9. The ducks (had) flown south for the winter.

10. An eagle (is) gliding through the sky.

11. The hawk (has) spotted a mouse.

12. A parrot (may) live for 80 years.

Try This

Accept reasonable responses.

Write four sentences about your day at school, using main and helping verbs. Circle the helping verbs. Underline the main verbs.

▲ Circle the helping verbs, and underline the main verbs.

1. I did not watch the sunset.

2. We will now change into pajamas.

3. I could not see the moon.

4. It was hidden behind a cloud.

5. They would not go to bed.

6. The baby has never slept through the night.

7. The dogs were already sleeping.

8. Stars are shining in the sky.

▲ Rewrite each sentence, using a helping verb from the box.

is	does	can	have

9. Moths _____ fly up to 25 miles per hour.

Moths can fly up to 25 miles per hour.

10. That moth _____ not have spots on its wings.

That moth does not have spots on its wings.

11. The butterfly _____ walking on a leaf.

The butterfly is walking on a leaf.

12. Those butterflies _____ gone to Mexico for the winter.

Those butterflies have gone to Mexico for the winter.

▲ Read this part of a student's rough draft. Then answer the questions that follow.

(1) In her dreams, Mandy can fly. (2) She gliding over the city at night. (3) The sun have set. (4) It will soon become dark. (5) Mandy loves her dream. (6) She will forget it.

1. Which has a helping verb that does NOT agree with the subject?
   A Sentence 1
   B Sentence 2
   C Sentence 3
   D Sentence 4

2. Which has a main verb and a helping verb used correctly?
   A Sentence 1
   B Sentence 2
   C Sentence 3
   D Sentence 5

3. The word *not* should follow the helping verb in Sentence 6. Where should it go?
   A after *She*
   B after *will*
   C after *forget*
   D after *it*

4. In which sentence should the helping verb *is* go before the main verb?
   A Sentence 2
   B Sentence 4
   C Sentence 5
   D Sentence 6

5. Which does NOT have a helping verb?
   A Sentence 1
   B Sentence 4
   C Sentence 5
   D Sentence 6

6. Which are the main and helping verbs in Sentence 4?
   A *will* and *soon*
   B *will* and *become*
   C *soon* and *become*
   D *become* and *dark*

Name

▲ Rewrite the sentences. Add a helping verb to each one. **Possible responses are shown.**

1. I never studied mammals.
   I have never studied mammals.

2. We learn about bats.
   We will learn about bats.

3. We go to the library.
   We should go to the library.

4. Butterflies see red, yellow, and green.
   Butterflies can see red, yellow, and green.

5. A butterfly landed on that leaf.
   A butterfly has landed on that leaf.

6. That butterfly laid 400 eggs.
   That butterfly has laid 400 eggs.

7. Butterflies fly only when they are warm.
   Butterflies will fly only when they are warm.

8. The librarian found a great book about butterflies.
   The librarian has found a great book about butterflies.

Main and
Helping Verbs
Lesson 22

Name

▲ Rewrite each sentence. Use the correct present-tense form of the verb in parentheses ( ).

1. I (help) my family.
   I help my family.

2. My sister (plant) carrot seeds.
   My sister plants carrot seeds.

3. We (work) together in the garden.
   We work together in the garden.

4. My brother (pick) tomatoes.
   My brother picks tomatoes.

5. My mother (carry) them inside.
   My mother carries them inside.

6. My father (wash) the tomatoes.
   My father washes the tomatoes.

7. He (slice) them into small pieces.
   He slices them into small pieces.

8. I (make) a salad for dinner.
   I make a salad for dinner.

9. A friend (eat) with us.
   A friend eats with us.

10. She (enjoy) the salad.
    She enjoys the salad.

Present-Tense
Verbs
Lesson 23

▲ Write the verb in each sentence. Then write *S* if the subject is singular or *P* if the subject is plural.

1. We plan a picnic. _____ plan, P

2. I make sandwiches. _____ make, S

3. A dish breaks. _____ breaks, S

4. Lila fixes it with glue. _____ fixes, S

5. The children eat under a tree. _____ eat, P

6. Teresa hears thunder. _____ hears, S

7. They put the food away. _____ put, P

8. She runs home. _____ runs, S

▲ Rewrite each sentence. Use the correct present-tense form of the verb in parentheses ( ).

9. Leah (like) this book.
   Leah likes this book.

10. The prince (marry) the princess.
    The prince marries the princess.

11. He (write) a fairy tale.
    He writes a fairy tale.

12. We (enjoy) the story.
    We enjoy the story.

▲ Read this part of a student's rough draft. Then answer the questions that follow.

(1) My father and I make a cake for my brother's birthday. (2) I mix the ingredients. (3) My father bake the cake in the oven. (4) We ices it together. (5) My brother _____ the cake at his party. (6) _____ loves it.

1. Which sentence has a singular subject and a correct present-tense verb?
   A Sentence 1
   B Sentence 2
   C Sentence 3
   D Sentence 4

2. Which sentence has a singular subject and an incorrect present-tense verb?
   A Sentence 1
   B Sentence 2
   C Sentence 3
   D Sentence 4

3. Which sentence has a plural subject and a correct present-tense verb?
   A Sentence 1
   B Sentence 2
   C Sentence 3
   D Sentence 4

4. Which sentence has a plural subject and an incorrect present-tense verb?
   A Sentence 1
   B Sentence 2
   C Sentence 3
   D Sentence 4

5. Which is a present-tense verb that could fill in the blank in Sentence 5?
   A eating
   B eat
   C eats
   D ate

6. Which subject could fill in the blank in Sentence 6?
   A He
   B We
   C He and his friends
   D My brother's friends

Name _____

▲ Rewrite each sentence correctly, using the subject in parentheses ( ). Be sure that the verb in your sentence agrees with its new subject.

Example: Glenda likes math. (My brothers)

My brothers like math.

1. I enter a writing contest. (George)

   George enters a writing contest.

2. The teachers judge the contest. (A teacher)

   A teacher judges the contest.

3. One student wins the contest. (Two students)

   Two students win the contest.

4. We like stories about animals. (You)

   You like stories about animals.

5. She prefers true stories. (He)

   He prefers true stories.

6. The princesses meet a prince. (The princess)

   The princess meets a prince.

7. We hurry home from school. (They)

   They hurry home from school.

8. Our mother opens the front door. (We)

   We open the front door.

Name _____

▲ Write the verb in each sentence. Then label it as *present, past,* or *future* tense.

1. Jen finishes her homework quickly.

   finishes; present

2. Simon will write an essay next week.

   will write; future

3. The teacher assigned five math problems.

   assigned; past

4. You carried a dictionary to school.

   carried; past

5. Students will read their reports aloud.

   will read; future

6. Jason draws a picture in art class.

   draws; present

7. We tried the science experiment at home.

   tried; past

8. The children named three kinds of plants.

   named; past

9. My sister learns Spanish in high school.

   learns; present

10. I will ask my mother for help.

    will ask; future

Past-Tense and
Future-Tense Verbs
Lesson 24

▲ Rewrite each sentence. Use the future-tense form of the verb in parentheses ( ).

1. Yolanda (stay) home from school today.
   Yolanda will stay home from school today.

2. She (go) to the doctor later.
   She will go to the doctor later.

3. The doctor (give) her some medicine.
   The doctor will give her some medicine.

4. She (feel) much better tomorrow.
   She will feel much better tomorrow.

▲ Write a sentence that uses the future-tense form of the verb.
Possible responses are shown.

5. run
   I will run in the park.

6. play
   Melissa will play with her friend.

7. hurry
   My mother will hurry home.

8. watch
   We will watch a movie later.

Grammar–Writing
Connection
Lesson 24

▲ Read this part of a student's rough draft. Then answer the questions that follow.

(1) Paul _____ all week for today's math test. (2) Soon he take the test. (3) He clears his desk. (4) His teacher hands him the test sheet. (5) She smiles and says "Good luck." (6) Paul worked hard, and he will do well on the test.

1. Which verb form BEST completes Sentence 1?
   A study
   B will study
   Ⓒ studied
   D studies

2. Which verb needs the helping verb *will* to make it a correct future-tense verb?
   Ⓐ take (Sentence 2)
   B clears (Sentence 3)
   C smiles (Sentence 5)
   D worked (Sentence 6)

3. Which sentence does NOT have a present-tense verb?
   A Sentence 3
   B Sentence 4
   C Sentence 5
   Ⓓ Sentence 6

4. Which sentence has two correct present-tense verbs?
   A Sentence 3
   B Sentence 4
   Ⓒ Sentence 5
   D Sentence 6

5. Which sentence has a correct past-tense verb?
   A Sentence 2
   B Sentence 3
   C Sentence 5
   Ⓓ Sentence 6

6. Which sentence has a correct future-tense verb?
   A Sentence 3
   B Sentence 4
   C Sentence 5
   Ⓓ Sentence 6

Name _____

Past-Tense and Future-Tense Verbs
Lesson 24

▲ Underline the verb in each sentence. Then rewrite the sentence in the tense shown in parentheses ( ).

1. The children study quietly. (past)
   The children studied quietly.

2. The teacher will talk about the report. (past)
   The teacher talked about the report.

3. Many students enjoyed music class. (present)
   Many students enjoy music class.

4. Mr. Green scores the test. (future)
   Mr. Green will score the test.

5. Tim will hurry to school. (present)
   Tim hurries to school.

6. We play outside during recess. (past)
   We played outside during recess.

7. You solved the math problem. (future)
   You will solve the math problem.

8. Misha practices the flute. (past)
   Misha practiced the flute.

Name _____

Grammar-Writing Connection
Lesson 25

▲ Read this part of a student's rough draft. Then answer the questions that follow.

(1) Mia and Simon writing a story. (2) The story are about a robot. (3) The robot is funny. (4) It _____ say all sorts of things. (5) The children are excited. (6) They will show the story to their teacher.

1. Which sentence has a singular subject and the correct form of the verb *be?*
   A Sentence 2
   (B) Sentence 3
   C Sentence 5
   (D) Sentence 6

2. Which sentence has a plural subject and the correct form of the verb *be?*
   A Sentence 2
   B Sentence 3
   (C) Sentence 5
   D Sentence 6

3. Which sentence has a form of the verb *be* that does NOT agree with the subject?
   (A) Sentence 2
   B Sentence 3
   C Sentence 5
   D Sentence 6

4. Which helping verb should go before the main verb in Sentence 1?
   A have
   B will
   C can
   (D) are

5. Which helping verb could complete Sentence 4?
   A have
   B had
   (C) can
   D is

6. Which other helping verb could replace *will* in Sentence 6?
   A had
   (B) can
   C have
   D were

Name _____

▲ Rewrite each sentence. Use the verb and tense shown in parentheses ( ). **Possible reponses are shown.**

1. I _____ a spider yesterday. (*see*—past tense)

   I saw a spider yesterday.

2. The spider _____ home to its web. (*go*—past tense)

   The spider went home to its web.

3. Shondra _____ a pet spider. (*have*—past tense)

   Shondra had a pet spider.

4. Zack _____ that he likes spiders. (*say*—present tense)

   Zack says that he likes spiders.

5. A spider _____ several things to catch insects. (*do*—present tense)

   A spider does several things to catch insects.

6. A fly _____ to the spider's web. (*come*—present tense)

   A fly comes to the spider's web.

7. That spider _____ (*have*—present tense) a sticky web.

   That spider has a sticky web.

8. The spider _____ (*do*—past tense) its work quickly.

   The spider did its work quickly.

Name _____

▲ Read this part of a student's rough draft. Then answer the questions that follow.

(1) William loves space. (2) He looked at pictures of the sun and moon when he was younger. (3) Now he read books about the solar system. (4) He will learn about the planets. (5) He will studies space travel. (6) One day he will become an astronaut.

1. Which sentence has a correct past-tense verb?
   A Sentence 1
   B Sentence 2
   C Sentence 4
   D Sentence 5

2. Which sentence has a correct present-tense verb?
   A Sentence 1
   B Sentence 2
   C Sentence 3
   D Sentence 4

3. Which sentence has an incorrect form of a future-tense verb?
   A Sentence 2
   B Sentence 4
   C Sentence 5
   D Sentence 6

4. Which verb should end with an *s*?
   A *looked* (Sentence 2)
   B *read* (Sentence 3)
   C *learn* (Sentence 4)
   D *become* (Sentence 6)

5. Which is the future-tense form of the verb in Sentence 1?
   A love
   B will love
   C will loves
   D loved

6. Which is the past-tense form of the verb in Sentence 4?
   A learn
   B learns
   C can learn
   D learned

Name _____

▲ Rewrite each sentence, using the correct present-tense verb in parentheses ( ).

1. The tired pig (lies, lays) in the grass.
   The tired pig lies in the grass.

2. The sun (rises, raises) over the field.
   The sun rises over the field.

3. The farmer (sits, sets) her bucket on a stool.
   The farmer sets her bucket on a stool.

4. He (lies, lays) a blanket over the horse.
   He lays a blanket over the horse.

5. We (sit, set) together under an apple tree.
   We sit together under an apple tree.

▲ Rewrite each sentence. Use the past-tense form of the verb shown in parentheses ( ).

6. Gwen _____ in the sun all afternoon. (lie)
   Gwen lay in the sun all afternoon.

7. The children _____ early for school. (rise)
   The children rose early for school.

8. You _____ the eggs on the table. (set)
   You set the eggs on the table.

9. The hen _____ many eggs. (lay)
   The hen laid many eggs.

Grammar Practice Book
© Harcourt • Grade 3

Name _____

▲ Read this part of a student's rough draft. Then answer the questions that follow.

(1) The sun risen, and it was a beautiful morning. (2) Nathan _____ in the grass. (3) He watched as three deer came to the river. (4) Nathan saw the deer drink. (5) He say nothing, because he did not want to scare them. (6) When the deer had finished drinking, Nathan _____ to his feet and walked quietly home.

1. Which verb form could go in the blank in Sentence 2?
   A lays
   B laid
   C lain
   D lay (circled)

2. Which is the present-tense form of the verb *saw* in Sentence 4?
   A did seen
   B had seen
   C had see
   D sees (circled)

3. Which is a correct past-tense verb to replace the underlined verb in Sentence 5?
   A says
   B sayed
   C said (circled)
   D saying

4. Which verb needs the helping verb *had* before it?
   A risen (Sentence 1) (circled)
   B saw (Sentence 4)
   C drink (Sentence 4)
   D scare (Sentence 5)

5. Which are the present-tense forms of the verbs in Sentence 3?
   A watches, come (circled)
   B did watch, had come
   C had watched, had come
   D will watch, will come

6. Which verb form could go in the blank in Sentence 6?
   A rise
   B rose (circled)
   C raise
   D raised

Grammar Practice Book
© Harcourt • Grade 3

Irregular Verbs
Lesson 26

▲ Rewrite each sentence, using the verb tense in parentheses ( ).

1. The spider laid eggs. (present tense)

   The spider lays eggs.

2. I have two books on spiders. (past tense)

   I had two books on spiders.

3. The farmer's daughter had done her chores. (present tense)

   The farmer's daughter does her chores.

4. She sits at the kitchen table. (past tense)

   She sat at the kitchen table.

5. Her brother comes home from school. (past tense)

   Her brother came home from school.

6. He will say "giddyup" to the horse. (past tense)

   He said "giddyup" to the horse.

7. The neighbors raised their new flag. (present tense)

   The neighbors raise their new flag.

8. We saw many animals on the farm. (present tense)

   We see many animals on the farm.

Adverbs
Lesson 27

▲ Write the adverb in each sentence. Then write whether it tells *how, where,* or *when.*

1. Ants work together in colonies.   **together, how**

2. We saw an ant hill outside.   **outside, where**

3. I observed ants earlier.   **earlier, when**

4. You touched one ant gently.   **gently, how**

5. Soon the ants will dig a nest.   **Soon, when**

6. Some ants left a trail here.   **here, where**

7. The big ant moves slowly.   **slowly, how**

8. Wow, those ants go everywhere!   **everywhere, where**

9. The ants carefully carry a bread crumb.   **carefully, how**

10. Worker ants always care for their queen.   **always, when**

11. Now the ants walk in a line.   **Now, when**

12. Those ants live underground.   **underground, where**

Try This

Write three sentences about your day at school. Use an adverb in each sentence. One adverb should tell *how,* one should tell *where,* and one should tell *when.* **Accept reasonable responses.**

© Harcourt • Grade 3

***Student Edition* pp. 94–95**

Name _____

▲ Rewrite each sentence. Use the correct comparative form of the adverb in parentheses ( ).

1. This ant works (hard) than that ant.
   This ant works harder than that ant.

2. Which butterfly flies the (low)?
   Which butterfly flies the lowest?

3. The shark swims (fast) than the fish.
   The shark swims faster than the fish.

4. That dolphin jumps the (high) of all.
   That dolphin jumps the highest of all.

5. These birds will fly south (soon) than those birds.
   These birds will fly south sooner than those birds.

▲ Rewrite each sentence. Add *more* or *the most* before the adverb.

6. The nightingale sings _____ beautifully of all the birds.
   The nightingale sings the most beautifully of all the birds.

7. A tiger moves _____ quietly than an elephant.
   A tiger moves more quietly than an elephant.

8. The horse drinks _____ often than the camel.
   The horse drinks more often than the camel.

9. My dog wags its tail _____ happily of all.
   My dog wags its tail the most happily of all.

Grammar Practice Book
© Harcourt • Grade 3

Name _____

▲ Read this part of a student's rough draft. Then answer the questions that follow.

> (1) I like science, and I work hard. (2) Yesterday I read about spiders. (3) Today I studied the planets. (4) I learned that Earth spins _____ than Mercury. (5) I also learned that Mercury moves around the sun _____ of all the planets. (6) I will visit a science museum soon, and I will learn more there.

1. Which word does the adverb in Sentence 1 describe?
   A I
   B like
   C science
   (D) work

2. Which sentence has an adverb that tells *how?*
   (A) Sentence 1
   B Sentence 2
   C Sentence 3
   D Sentence 6

3. Which sentence has an adverb that tells *where?*
   A Sentence 1
   B Sentence 2
   C Sentence 3
   (D) Sentence 6

4. Which sentence does NOT have an adverb that tells *when?*
   (A) Sentence 1
   B Sentence 2
   C Sentence 3
   D Sentence 6

5. Which form of an adverb could go in the blank in Sentence 4?
   A fast
   (B) faster
   C more faster
   D fastest

6. Which form of an adverb could go in the blank in Sentence 5?
   A quick
   B quickly
   (C) most quickly
   D more quickly

Grammar Practice Book
© Harcourt • Grade 3

Name _____

▲ Write the adverb in each sentence. Then write the verb that it describes.

1. My teacher talks excitedly about science.

   excitedly, talks

2. Tomorrow we will learn about insects.

   Tomorrow, learn (will learn)

3. Of all the students, Evan studied the longest.

   the longest, studied

4. I speak more softly than the other students at the library.

   more softly, speak

▲ Rewrite each sentence. Complete it with an adverb that answers the question in parentheses ( ).
Possible responses are shown.

5. This spider crawls _____ than that spider. (How?)

   This spider crawls more quickly than that spider.

6. I put my report _____. (Where?)

   I put my report there.

7. _____ you will learn about the sun. (When?)

   Now you will learn about the sun.

Grammar Practice Book
© Harcourt • Grade 3

Name _____

▲ Rewrite each sentence. Replace the underlined words with a contraction.

1. It is an exciting day.

   It's an exciting day.

2. I am going to be in a baking contest.

   I'm going to be in a baking contest.

3. Some children did not know about the contest.

   Some children didn't know about the contest.

4. You are bringing two pies.

   You're bringing two pies.

5. My brothers are not baking anything.

   My brothers aren't baking anything.

6. They had not entered the contest.

   They hadn't entered the contest.

7. The judges were not in the room.

   The judges weren't in the room.

8. They are eager to taste my cookies.

   They're eager to taste my cookies.

9. My father could not come to the contest.

   My father couldn't come to the contest.

10. We should not eat too much cake.

   We shouldn't eat too much cake.

Grammar Practice Book
© Harcourt • Grade 3

Name _____

▲ Rewrite each sentence, using the correct word(s) in parentheses ( ).

1. You hadn't (ever, never) told me about volcanoes.
   You hadn't ever told me about volcanoes.

2. I don't know (nothing, anything) about them.
   I don't know anything about them.

3. My brother hasn't won (any, no) science prizes yet.
   My brother hasn't won any science prizes yet.

4. My sister doesn't have (none, any) either.
   My sister doesn't have any either.

5. We haven't told (anybody, nobody) about the contest.
   We haven't told anybody about the contest.

6. Laurie wouldn't tell her friends (neither, either).
   Laurie wouldn't tell her friends either.

7. Carlos won't go (anywhere, nowhere) without a notebook.
   Carlos won't go anywhere without a notebook.

8. Isn't (no one, anyone) in the classroom?
   Isn't anyone in the classroom?

9. Those children never enter (any, no) contests.
   Those children never enter any contests.

10. No one said (nothing, anything) about cleaning up.
    No one said anything about cleaning up.

Name _____

▲ Read this part of a student's rough draft. Then answer the questions that follow.

(1) Maria is not going to give up! (2) She is making an electric buzzer for her science project. (3) She has not ever made one before, but her teacher showed her how. (4) Now Maria doesn't even need no help. (5) Maria's teacher smiles at her. (6) _____ glad that she's in his class.

1. Which sentence has a contraction that is formed with a pronoun?
   A Sentence 2
   B Sentence 4
   C Sentence 5
   D Sentence 6

2. Which sentence has a contraction that is formed with the word *not*?
   A Sentence 1
   B Sentence 4
   C Sentence 5
   D Sentence 6

3. Which sentence does NOT have two words that could form a contraction?
   A Sentence 1
   B Sentence 2
   C Sentence 3
   D Sentence 5

4. In which sentence could you form a contraction that includes a subject pronoun?
   A Sentence 1
   B Sentence 2
   C Sentence 4
   D Sentence 5

5. Which is a correct contraction that could go in the blank in Sentence 6?
   A He's
   B Hes'
   C He'd
   D He're

6. Which sentence has an error in it?
   A Sentence 2
   B Sentence 3
   C Sentence 4
   D Sentence 5

Name _____

▲ Rewrite each sentence. Replace each contraction with the words used to form it.

1. Alice doesn't see that we're waving.
   Alice does not see that we are waving.

2. She's worried that we haven't arrived.
   She is worried that we have not arrived.

3. I'm glad that you didn't stay home.
   I am glad that you did not stay home.

4. It isn't clear that he's the winner.
   It is not clear that he is the winner.

▲ If the sentence is correct, write *correct*. If it is not, rewrite it correctly.

5. Wouldn't you like any help?
   correct

6. I don't see my teacher nowhere.
   I don't see my teacher anywhere.

7. There wasn't nobody in the cafeteria.
   There wasn't anybody in the cafeteria.

Grammar Practice Book
© Harcourt • Grade 3

Name _____

▲ Rewrite each sentence. Use capital letters and commas correctly.

1. my father my sister and i watch the stars every night.
   My father, my sister, and I watch the stars every night.

2. we sit outside in june july and august.
   We sit outside in June, July, and August.

3. there is a telescope at school and i can use it.
   There is a telescope at school, and I can use it.

4. mrs. morgan helps us point the telescope toward mars.
   Mrs. Morgan helps us point the telescope toward Mars.

5. on monday we look at jupiter but on tuesday we look at saturn.
   On Monday we look at Jupiter, but on Tuesday we look at Saturn.

6. the sky is bright with fireworks on independence day.
   The sky is bright with fireworks on Independence Day.

7. i lie in the grass close my eyes and listen.
   I lie in the grass, close my eyes, and listen.

8. karen learns about the planets at lincoln elementary school.
   Karen learns about the planets at Lincoln Elementary School.

9. she reads books looks at pictures and asks questions.
   She reads books, looks at pictures, and asks questions.

10. students can watch a short movie or they can read quietly.
    Students can watch a short movie, or they can read quietly.

Grammar Practice Book
© Harcourt • Grade 3

© Harcourt • Grade 3

Student Edition pp. 102–103

Name _____

▲ Rewrite each title correctly. The words in parentheses ( ) tell what kind of title each one is.

1. Charlie and the Chocolate Factory (book)

   Charlie and the Chocolate Factory

2. In Which Piglet Is Entirely Surrounded by Water (chapter from a book)

   "In Which Piglet Is Entirely Surrounded by Water"

3. Hickory, Dickory, Dock (song)

   "Hickory, Dickory, Dock"

4. Ranger Rick (magazine)

   Ranger Rick

5. Lake Country Gazette (newspaper)

   Lake Country Gazette

▲ Rewrite each sentence. Write titles correctly.

6. Have you read the book Little House on the Prairie?

   Have you read the book Little House on the Prairie?

7. My little sister likes the song Three Blind Mice.

   My little sister likes the song "Three Blind Mice."

8. Robert Louis Stevenson wrote a poem called The Lamplighter.

   Robert Louis Stevenson wrote a poem called "The Lamplighter."

9. Students Speak is a column in our school newspaper.

   "Students Speak" is a column in our school newspaper.

Name _____

▲ Read this part of a student's rough draft. Then answer the questions that follow.

(1) Mr. mercado is my neighbor and he knows a lot about the stars. (2) he gave me a book called he find the constellations. (3) My brother my best friend and i read the book together. (4) We learned that there is a group of stars named Ursa Major. (5) they are supposed to look like a bear but they just look like pretty stars to me.

1. Which sentence is NOT missing one or more commas?
   - A Sentence 1
   - Ⓑ Sentence 2
   - C Sentence 3
   - D Sentence 5

2. Which sentence needs two commas?
   - A Sentence 1
   - B Sentence 2
   - Ⓒ Sentence 3
   - D Sentence 5

3. Which sentence has a proper noun that should be capitalized?
   - Ⓐ Sentence 1
   - B Sentence 3
   - C Sentence 4
   - D Sentence 5

4. Which sentence does NOT have a pronoun that should be capitalized?
   - Ⓐ Sentence 1
   - B Sentence 2
   - C Sentence 3
   - D Sentence 5

5. Which sentence has a title that should be capitalized and underlined?
   - A Sentence 1
   - Ⓑ Sentence 2
   - C Sentence 3
   - D Sentence 4

6. Which sentence has a correct proper noun?
   - A Sentence 1
   - B Sentence 2
   - C Sentence 3
   - Ⓓ Sentence 4

▲ Rewrite each sentence correctly.

1. sometimes i sing my favorite song.

Sometimes I sing my favorite song.

2. that song is called twinkle, twinkle, little star.

That song is called "Twinkle, Twinkle, Little Star."

3. those three stars are named altair castor and polaris.

Those three stars are named Altair, Castor, and Polaris.

4. sirius is the brightest star in the sky and i see it at night.

Sirius is the brightest star in the sky, and I see it at night.

5. you can read about stars in a magazine called Ask.

You can read about stars in a magazine called Ask.

6. mrs. wong reads to children at the library in middletown.

Mrs. Wong reads to children at the library in Middletown.

7. she lives in new york but she works in connecticut.

She lives in New York, but she works in Connecticut.

8. today she reads the book a child's introduction to the night sky.

Today she reads the book A Child's Introduction to the Night Sky.

▲ Read this part of a student's rough draft. Then answer the questions that follow.

(1) Yesterday my class went to an animal park. (2) We saw lions from the window of the school bus. (3) One lion _____ on a rock. (4) Monkeys played happily in the trees. (5) Some of them come excitedly to the bus. (6) _____, I will write a story about all the animals I seen.

1. Which of these verb forms could go in the blank in Sentence 3?
   A sit
   B sets
   C sat
   D set

2. Which verb needs the helping verb *have* before it?
   A went (Sentence 1)
   B saw (Sentence 2)
   C write (Sentence 6)
   D seen (Sentence 6)

3. Which is the past-tense form that could replace the underlined verb in Sentence 5?
   A comes
   B comed
   C came
   D camed

4. Which sentence has an adverb that tells *when*?
   A Sentence 1
   B Sentence 2
   C Sentence 4
   D Sentence 5

5. Which sentence does NOT have an adverb?
   A Sentence 1
   B Sentence 2
   C Sentence 4
   D Sentence 5

6. Which adverb could go in the blank in Sentence 6?
   A Tomorrow
   B More quickly
   C Most slowly
   D More slow

Name _____

Grammar–Writing
Connection
Lesson 30

▲ **Read this part of a student's rough draft. Then answer the questions that follow.**

(1) Latisha, Latisha's father and his friend went to Tonto National Forest in Arizona. (2) They _____ stay long but they had a great time. (3) They camped, hiked and swam on friday. (4) On Saturday night they sang a song around the campfire called "Make New Friends." (5) Latisha didn't never want to leave the forest.

1. Which sentence has a contraction?
   A Sentence 1
   B Sentence 3
   C Sentence 4
   D Sentence 5

2. Which contraction could go in the blank in Sentence 2?
   A doesn't
   B aren't
   C couldn't
   D they're

3. Which sentence has a double negative that needs to be corrected?
   A Sentence 1
   B Sentence 3
   C Sentence 4
   D Sentence 5

4. Which of these sentences does NOT need a comma added?
   A Sentence 1
   B Sentence 2
   C Sentence 3
   D Sentence 5

5. Which of these sentences has a proper noun that is incorrect?
   A Sentence 1
   B Sentence 3
   C Sentence 4
   D Sentence 5

6. Which sentence is correct?
   A Sentence 1
   B Sentence 3
   C Sentence 4
   D Sentence 5